To the party
of the first part—
I love you.
The party of the
second part.

To _____

From _____

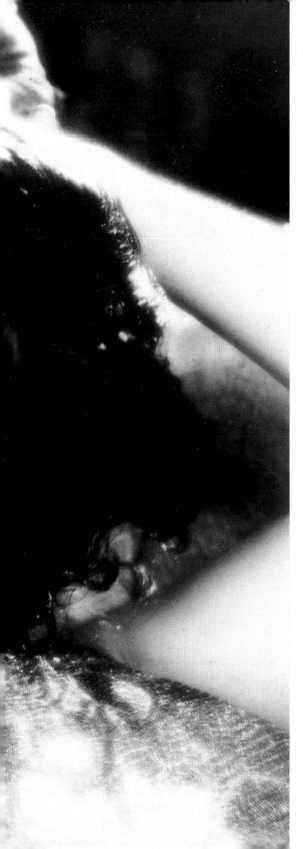

FLESH AND THE DEVIL *Greta Garbo and John Gilbert 1926*

KISSES

EDITED BY
LENA TABORI

Citadel Press

Turner Publishing, Inc.

A few thanks:

To Michael Reagan who said Yes, again and again. To Ira Miskin for having the good sense (and good humor) to underscore the Yes by commissioning a *Kisses* special for TBS. To Roger Mayer whose courtliness and loyalty to the MGM library are legendary and true. To Dick May and Cathy Manolis whose warmth and welcome belie the ferocity, professionalism and willingness with which they protect the fragile and irreplaceable films within the TEC archives. To Richard Ackerman, our invaluable guide to that extraordinary resource, our loyal critic, our ever-responsive information bank. To Robert Cushman at the Academy Foundation who watches over the MGM Special Collection. To Mary Tiegreen, the zany, the charming, the Myrna Loy of the design world who, from the beginning, had an unreasonable faith that it would all work in the end. To Natasha Tabori Fried who, despite being my daughter, had the courage to handle the day-to-day editorial work making certain that each road taken was well charted. To Hiro Clark, who brings grace to reliability, all the time. Finally, to the screenwriters and lyricists who wrote the extraordinary words, only a few of which can be reproduced here, and to the photographers who created these utterly delicious photographs.

—Lena Tabori

A Citadel Press/Turner Publishing Book
January 1991

For information address:
Carol Publishing Group, 120 Enterprise Avenue, Secaucus, NJ 07094
Produced by:
Welcome Enterprises, Inc., 164 East 95 Street, New York, NY 10128
Library of Congress Cataloging-in-Publication-Data
Kisses / edited by Lena Tabori
p.   cm.
"A Citadel Press/Turner Publishing Book "
ISBN 0-8065-9000-9 (cloth) : $22.50
1. Kissing in motion pictures.   2. Love in motion pictures.
3. Motion pictures—History.   I. Tabori, Lena.
PN1995.9.K57K58   1990   90-47517
791.43′6538—dc20   CIP

Printed and bound in Italy

CONTENTS

INTRODUCTION

I was born to a film star. Her name is Viveca Lindfors. She kissed on screen. And off. One of my earliest memories is coming into the kitchen and finding my mother and stepfather kissing. It made me proud to "catch" my parents doing such an intimate thing. Few of my friends had that experience. But, we all went to the movies and in the darkness we watched people kissing. Well, most of us did. In Italy, during a certain period and in a certain town, the kissing scenes were cut from the films before they were screened. At least that's what *Cinema Paradiso* would have us believe. Of course, in that film they thought kissing was about sex. When we were young, we all thought kissing was about love.

Last year, Michael Reagan—newly named Vice President in charge of Publishing for Turner Broadcasting System—asked me to visit their film archives in Los Angeles. I went there to begin thinking about the kind of publishing projects which might be developed from the extraordinary assets acquired over the past years by Ted Turner.

For anyone still sorting fantasy from reality, it was a place to be lost forever. All the MGM films were there, pre-1948 Warner and

RKO, even United Artists. And, there too, were the photo stills, stacked in boxes, one atop the other, in rows which went on as far as the eye could see: *Gone With the Wind, Some Like It Hot, Tarzan, Tom & Jerry* written in big black letters on the sides. Inside the boxes: Greta Garbo (who made all her films for MGM), Fred Astaire and Ginger Rogers, Judy Garland and Mickey Rooney, Clark Gable and Joan Crawford, Myrna Loy and William Powell, Marilyn Monroe and Tony Curtis. Michael, a photographer, and I, a publisher, were gone. The riches were extraordinary. What seemed like days later, the guard let us out into the night. We were finally satisfied. We knew how we wanted to begin. Our list of potential titles covered pages. But *Kisses* was first.

I started looking at films, including every film someone recommended as having a special kiss. And I became newly astonished. They weren't always about love. There were also kisses of passion, of manipulation, of seduction, of friendship, of betrayal, of commitment, sadness, resignation, and amusement. The kisses in the movies were like kisses in life. They said "Hello" and "Goodbye." They said "Let's see" and "Forever." They were giving and demanding, dependent and autonomous, beginning a negotiation or sealing a deal. Rarely did my kissing couple

(LEFT)
SUSAN LENOX, HER FALL AND RISE
GRETA GARBO
AND
CLARK GABLE
1931

(ABOVE)
NIGHT UNTO NIGHT
RONALD REAGAN
AND
VIVECA LINDFORS
1949

say "I love you" before, during or after.

The book was gaining its own life (as all creative ideas do), growing from an idea into something defined and wonderful. Momentarily, I abandoned my passion for the photographers, throwing in my lot with the lyricists and writers. For awhile, they were my greatest allies, providing surprising, delicious and wondrous words.

Of course, in the end, there needed to be a marriage of all these, and, of course, there was. This book is the result.

—Lena Tabori, 8-23-90

BOLERO
GEORGE RAFT AND CAROLE LOMBARD
1934

ADVICE TO THOSE IN LOVE

CHAPTER ONE

INNOCENCE

"Yes, I love him. I love the hick shirts he wears and the boiled cuffs and the way he always has his vest buttoned wrong. He looks like a giraffe, and I love him. I love him because he's the kind of guy who gets drunk on a glass of buttermilk, and I love the way he blushes right up over his ears. I love him because he doesn't know how to kiss—the jerk! I love him, Joe. That's what I'm trying to tell ya."

—Barbara Stanwyck
as Sugarpuss

Shirley

Never liked a copycat
Or the things they do,
But it seems that you
Must have changed my mind.

Daddy

Me?

* * *

I like what you like—
Beans and oyster stew—
And I like what you like
On account of I love you.

they kiss

You're my chocolate sundae,
You're my sugarbun,
Apple pie and lollipop,
All rolled into one.

* * *

Shirley

Yes, you.
I became a copycat,
And I love it, too.
All the things you go for
Are the things I go for.

I go where you go—
Any place will do—
And I go where you go
On account of I love you.

they kiss

I say what you say,
Even black is blue,
And I'll say what you say
On account of I love you.

they kiss

BABY TAKE A BOW
JAMES DUNN AND SHIRLEY TEMPLE
1934

DANNY:

Did I ever tell you that a fella in my state of mind is apt to kiss a girl in your state of mind?

GINGER:

I dare you.

DANNY:
You what?

GINGER:

I double dare you.

—Mickey Rooney
and Judy Garland
in *Girl Crazy*

TOMMY:

Penny, did you ever find someone and then all of a sudden you felt like you were taking off
right out into space, like a propeller going round and round and round,
thirty thousand revolutions a minute, and there wasn't any landing fields left in the world?

PENNY:

Uh-huh, I've had that feeling, and it all started in a drugstore.

TOMMY:

Penny!

PENNY:

Yeah.
(they kiss)

PENNY:

Tommy!

TOMMY:

Oh, isn't it wonderful what you can find these days in drugstores?

BABES ON BROADWAY

JUDY GARLAND AND MICKEY ROONEY
1941

*"A girl
should never kiss
a man
she doesn't
intend to marry."*

—Judy Garland as Nellie,
LITTLE NELLIE KELLY

(LEFT)
ZIEGFELD GIRL
JACKIE COOPER AND JUDY GARLAND
1941

(RIGHT)
LITTLE NELLIE KELLY
DOUGLAS MCPHAIL,
JUDY GARLAND, AND GEORGE MURPHY
1940

<big>T</big>here's honey in the honeycomb,
There's nectar in the peach,
There's candy in a coconut shell
And mussels on every beach.
Oh, there's money in the savings bank
And I'll personally guarantee
If there's honey in the honeycomb
Then baby, look out, there's love in me.
Oh, there's honey in the honeycomb
And, baby, there's love, love,
Baby, there's love in me.

CABIN IN THE SKY
ETHEL WATERS AND JOHN W. "BUBBLES" BUBLETT
1943

(they kiss)

• JERRY •

Oooh! My head's going like a pinwheel!

• TED •

My heart's beating like a steam engine. Feel.

• JERRY •

When did you first start having heart trouble?

• TED •

From the first moment I met you.

THE DIVORCEE

CHESTER MORRIS AND NORMA SHEARER
1930

PAULA:

Darling, you've proposed to me, and I've accepted you . . .

CHARLES:

What's wrong? What's wrong?

PAULA:

Smithy, do I always have to take the initiative?
You're supposed to kiss me, darling.

CHARLES:

Oh, my.

(they kiss)

RANDOM HARVEST
RONALD COLMAN AND GREER GARSON
1942

TARZAN:
Good morning. I love you.

Jane:
Good morning. I love you.
You never forget, do you, Tarzan?

TARZAN:
Never forget I love you.

Jane:
Love who?

TARZAN:
Love you.

Jane:
Love who?

TARZAN:
Love Jane.

Jane:
Love my . . .

TARZAN:
Love my . . . ? Wife! My wife.

(they kiss)

(LEFT)
TARZAN AND HIS MATE
MAUREEN O'SULLIVAN
AND
JOHNNY WEISSMULLER
1934

(RIGHT)
TARZAN ESCAPES
JOHNNY WEISSMULLER
AND
MAUREEN O'SULLIVAN
1936

ROMEO
If I profane with my unworthiest hand this holy shrine, the gentle fine is this:
my lips, two blushing pilgrims, ready stand to smooth that rough touch
with a tender kiss.

JULIET
Good pilgrim, you do wrong your hand too much, for saints hath hands
that pilgrims' hands do touch,
and palm to palm, is holy palmers' kiss.

ROMEO
Have not saints lips, and holy palmers, too?

JULIET
Ay, pilgrim, lips that they must use in prayer.

ROMEO
Oh, then, dear saint, let lips do what hands do; they pray; grant thou, lest faith turn to despair.

JULIET
Saints do not move, though grant for prayers' sake.

ROMEO
Then move not, while my prayer's effect I take.

(they kiss)

ROMEO
Thus from my lips, by thine, my sin is purged.

JULIET
Then have my lips the sin that they have took.

ROMEO
Sin from my lips? O trespass sweetly urged! Give me my sin again.

(they kiss)

ROMEO AND JULIET
LESLIE HOWARD AND NORMA SHEARER
1936

CHAPTER TWO

PASSION

"There's a 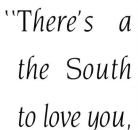 soldier of the South who wants to love you, Scarlett, who wants to feel your arms around him, who wants to carry the memory of your kisses into battle with him. Never mind about loving me. Scarlett, kiss me. Kiss me."

—Clark Gable as Rhett Butler

(LEFT)
THE POSTMAN ALWAYS RINGS TWICE
LANA TURNER AND JOHN GARFIELD
1946

(ABOVE)
GONE WITH THE WIND
CLARK GABLE AND VIVIEN LEIGH
1939

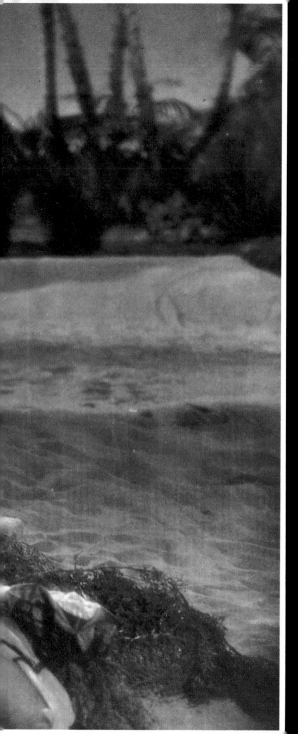

> *"When love is
> more desired than riches,
> it is the will of Allah."*
>
> —Rudolph Valentino,
> **THE SHEIK 1921**

THE SON OF THE SHEIK
**VILMA BANKY
AND
RUDOLPH VALENTINO**

LOLA:

But you hardly know me.

◆ ◆ ◆

GIFFORD:

've known you in every ripple of moonlight I've
ever seen, in every symphony I've ever heard, in
every perfume I've ever smelt. . . Your hair, your
hair is like a field of silver daisies. I'd like to run
barefoot through your hair.

◆ ◆ ◆

LOLA:

Gifford—you mustn't, Gifford.

◆ ◆ ◆

GIFFORD:

h but my dearest! Your mouth is like a gardenia
opening to the sun. Your lips. . .

BOMBSHELL
JEAN HARLOW AND FRANCHOT TONE

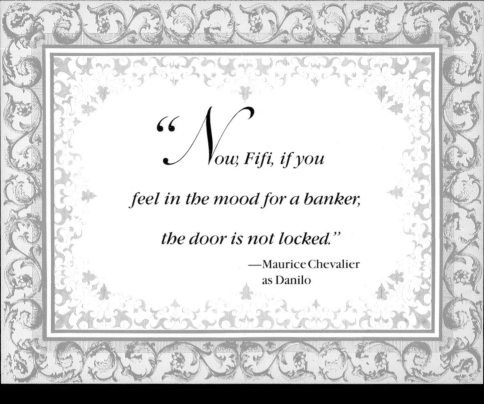

"*Now, Fifi, if you feel in the mood for a banker, the door is not locked.*"

—Maurice Chevalier
as Danilo

THE MERRY WIDOW
MAURICE CHEVALIER AND JEANETTE MACDONALD
1934

GREGORY:
What were you
dreaming of?

Paula:
Our life
together.

GREGORY:
And how do
you see it?

Paula:
I saw all
the places
where we'd
be together.
Lovely
places.

GREGORY:
I was thinking
of our life
together, too,
only I heard
it in music.
Something that
I want to write.

Paula:
Yes, what?

GREGORY:
The whole
thing is alive
with happiness.
I want a feeling
of the early
morning.

Paula:
This
morning.

GREGORY:
Yes, with the
sun rising in
your hair, as it
is now. I don't
know how it
ends. Perhaps
it never ends
until I write
you.

(they kiss)

GASLIGHT
INGRID BERGMAN AND CHARLES BOYER
1944

"**F**orget you? Not while I live . . .

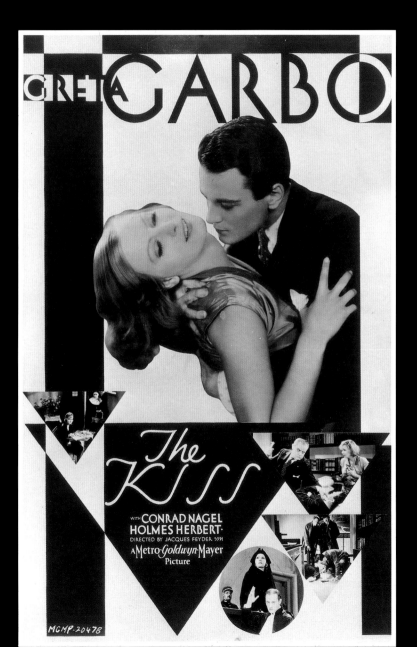

THE KISS
GRETA GARBO
AND
LEW AYRES
1929

. . .not if I die." —John Gilbert as Leo, *Flesh and the Devil*

(TOP LEFT)
**SUSAN LENOX,
HER FALL
AND RISE**
**GRETA GARBO
AND
CLARK GABLE
1931**

(TOP RIGHT)
CAMILLE
**ROBERT TAYLOR
AND
GRETA GARBO
1937**

(BOTTOM LEFT)
**A WOMAN
OF AFFAIRS**
**JOHN GILBERT
AND
GRETA GARBO
1928**

(BOTTOM RIGHT)
**FLESH
AND THE DEVIL**
**GRETA GARBO
AND
JOHN GILBERT
1926**

= ALEXIS: =

I love you as one adores sacred things.

= MATA: =

What sacred things?

= ALEXIS: =

God, country, honor, you.

= MATA: =

I come last?

= ALEXIS: =

No.

= MATA: =

That's how you said it.

= ALEXIS: =

You come first. Before anything.

= MATA: =

Before anything?

= ALEXIS: =

Yes.

(they kiss just barely)

= MATA: =

There's so much light in here. (indicates
a candle) Put out that one, too.

= ALEXIS: =

The Madonna's lamp?

= MATA: =

Yes.

= ALEXIS: =

I can't do that.

= MATA: =

You said I came first.

= ALEXIS: =

You don't understand. That's the holy
lamp. I swore to keep it burning.

= MATA: =

You wouldn't do that for me?

= ALEXIS: =

Why? Why do you ask me to?

= MATA: =

To see if you love me as you say.

= ALEXIS: =

I do. But I do.

= MATA: =

Then put it out if you love me.

= ALEXIS: =

I'll do anything, but please don't ask me
to do that.

= MATA: =

I'm going.

= ALEXIS: =

No!

*(he gets up, goes to the candle, looks at
her, and looks at the candle)*

= ALEXIS =
(to the statue):
Forgive me.

(he blows it out)

MATA HARI
GRETA GARBO AND RAMON NOVARRO
1931

ARMAND

I'll love you all my life.

I know that now.

All my life.

CHRISTINA:
*I have imagined happiness…
happiness you cannot imagine…
happiness you must feel, joy you must
feel. Oh, this great joy I feel now!
Antonio!*

ANTONIO:
What?

CHRISTINA:
*This is how the Lord must have felt
when he first beheld the finished
world with all his creatures breath-
ing, living…
(they kiss)*

ANTONIO:
*And to think a few snowdrifts might
have separated us forever.*

QUEEN CHRISTINA
GRETA GARBO AND JOHN GILBERT
1933

> *T*hink how many times the
> lady with the camellias has lured
> her admirers on to become
> the victims of
> her seductive wiles!
>
> —Dialogue Card

CAMILLE
ALLA NAZIMOVA AND RUDOLPH VALENTINO
1921

MADAME BOVARY
JENNIFER JONES AND LOUIS JOURDAN
1949

"This face that haunts me, drugs me . . . these hands that were designed for a thousand pleasures . . . these lips . . . were they meant to speak of love or grocery lists?"

—Louis Jourdan
as Rodolphe

ANTONY:

*Tell me. Tell me, how many have loved you
since him? One? Ten? No one? Have
they kissed you with Caesar's lips? Touched
you with his hands? Has it been his name
you've cried out in the dark, and afterward,
alone, has he reproached you, and have
you begged forgiveness of his memory?*

CLEOPATRA:

*You come here, then, running over with
wine and self-pity to conquer Caesar.*

ANTONY:

*So long now, you've filled my life. Like a
great noise that I hear everywhere in my
heart. I want to be free of you, of wanting
you, of being afraid . . .*

CLEOPATRA:

That Caesar would not permit it.

*(he rips Caesar's necklace from her neck,
and they kiss)*

ANTONY:

But I will never be free of you.

ASHLEY: *Oh please, Scarlett, please. You mustn't cry. Please, my brave dear. You mustn't.*
(they kiss)

SCARLETT: *You do love me! You do love me!*

ASHLEY: *Don't.*

SCARLETT: *You do love me!*

ASHLEY: *We won't do this, I tell you. We won't do this! It won't happen again.*

GONE WITH THE WIND
LESLIE HOWARD
AND
VIVIEN LEIGH
1939

RHETT: *There's one thing I do know, and that is that I love you, Scarlett. In spite of you and me and the whole silly world going to pieces around us, I love you, because we're alike—bad lots, both of us. Selfish and true and able to look things in the eye and call them by their right names.*

SCARLETT: *Don't hold me like that.*

RHETT: *Scarlett, look at me. I love you more than I've ever loved any woman. I've waited for you longer than I've ever waited for any woman. (he kisses her forehead)*

SCARLETT: *Let me alone.*

GONE WITH THE WIND
CLARK GABLE
AND
VIVIEN LEIGH
1939

SCARLETT: *You're a fool, Rhett Butler, when you know I shall always love another man.*

RHETT: *Stop it. Do you hear me, Scarlett? Stop it! No more of that talk! (he kisses her)*

SCARLETT: *Rhett, don't. I shall faint.*

RHETT: *I want you to faint. That's what you were meant for. None of the fools you've ever known have kissed you like this, have they? Your Charles or your Frank or your stupid Ashley! (they kiss)*

RHETT: *Say you're going to marry me. Say yes. Say it.*

SCARLETT: *Yes.*

RHETT: *Are you sure you meant it? You don't want to take it back?*

SCARLETT: *No.*

RHETT: *Look at me and try to tell me the truth. Did you say yes because of my money?*

SCARLETT: *Well, yes. Partly.*

GONE WITH THE WIND
CLARK GABLE AND VIVIEN LEIGH
1939

EVE: I'm a big girl.
THORNHILL: Yeah, and in all the
   right places, too.
   (they kiss)
EVE: You know, this is ridiculous.
   You know that, don't you?
THORNHILL: Yes.
EVE: I mean, we've hardly met.
THORNHILL: That's right.
EVE: How do I know you aren't a
   murderer?
THORNHILL: You don't.
EVE: Maybe you're planning
   to murder me right here
   tonight.
THORNHILL: Should I?
EVE: Please do.
   (they kiss)

(later)
EVE: I ought to know more about
   you.
THORNHILL: Well, what more
   could you know?
   (they kiss)
EVE: You're an advertising man.
   That's all I know.
THORNHILL: That's right . . .
   Train's a little unsteady.
EVE: Who isn't?
THORNHILL: What else do you
   know?
   (they kiss)

EVE: You've got taste in clothes,
   taste in food . . .
   (they kiss)
THORNHILL: And taste in
   women. I like your flavor.
   (they kiss)
EVE: You're very clever with
   murderers. You can
   probably make them do
   anything for you.
   (they kiss)
EVE: . . . sell people things they
   don't need, make women
   who don't love you fall in
   love with you . . .
   (they kiss)
THORNHILL: I'm beginning to
   think I'm underpaid.
   (they kiss)

NORTH BY NORTHWEST
CARY GRANT AND EVA MARIE SAINT
1959

“**O**h, now don’t turn ordinary on me. I get tired of ordinary dames, and I don’t want to ever get tired of you.”

—Robert Taylor
as Johnny Eager

(they kiss)

KAREN: I never knew it could be like this. Nobody ever kissed me the way you do.

WARDEN: Nobody?

KAREN: No, nobody.

WARDEN: Not even one, out of all the men you've been kissed by?

KAREN: Now, that'd take some figuring. How many do you think there have been?

WARDEN: I wouldn't know. Can't you give me a rough estimate?

KAREN: Not without an adding machine. Do you have your adding machine with you?

WARDEN: I forgot to bring it.

KAREN: Then I guess you won't find out, will you?
(later)

WARDEN: Karen. Listen to me. Listen . . .

KAREN: I know. Until I met you, I didn't think it was possible either.

FROM HERE TO ETERNITY
DEBORAH KERR AND BURT LANCASTER
1953

THE MERRY WIDOW
MAE MURRAY
AND
JOHN GILBERT
1925

DANCING IN THE DARK

TILL THE TUNE ENDS

WE'RE DANCING IN THE DARK

AND IT SOON ENDS;

WE'RE WALTZING IN THE WONDER
OF WHY WE'RE HERE

TIME HURRIES BY

WE'RE HERE AND GONE

LOOKING FOR THE LIGHT OF A NEW LOVE
TO BRIGHTEN THE NIGHT

I HAVE YOU, LOVE

AND WE CAN FACE
THE MUSIC TOGETHER

DANCING IN THE DARK

—from THE BANDWAGON

THE BANDWAGON
FRED ASTAIRE
AND
CYD CHARISSE
1953

SINGIN' IN THE RAIN
GENE KELLY
AND
CYD CHARISSE
1952

"Oh, Honnnnnnnnney!"

—Lena Horne
as Georgia

SUGAR

Have you ever tried American girls?

JOE

Why?

(they kiss)

SUGAR

Was it anything?

JOE

I'm not quite sure. Can we try it again?

(they kiss)

JOE

*I've got a funny sensation in my toes,
like someone was barbecuing them over
a slow flame.*

SUGAR

Let's throw another log on the fire.

(they kiss)

JOE

I think you're on the right track.

SUGAR

*I must be. Your glasses are beginning to
steam up.*

(they kiss)

JOE
I never knew it could be like this.

(He removes his glasses.)

SUGAR
Thank you.

JOE
They told me I was kaput, finished, all washed up. And here you are making a chump out of all those experts . . . Where did you learn to kiss like that?

SUGAR
I used to sell kisses for the milk fund.

(they kiss)

JOE
Tomorrow, remind me to send a check for a hundred thousand dollars to the milk fund.

(Much later)

JOE
How much do I owe the milk fund so far?

SUGAR
Eight hundred and fifty thousand dollars.

SOME LIKE IT HOT
TONY CURTIS AND MARILYN MONROE
1959

MARIE: You know, Steve, you're not very hard to figure. Only at

times. Sometimes, I know exactly what you're going to say.

The other times . . . (She sits in his lap.) The other times, you're

just a stinker. (they kiss) **STEVE:** What did you do that for?

MARIE: I'm wondering if I'd like it. **STEVE:** What's the decision?

MARIE: I don't know yet. (they kiss) **MARIE:** It's even better

when you help.

TO HAVE AND HAVE NOT
LAUREN BACALL AND HUMPHREY BOGART
1945

"I never wanted
to see you again.
But you pulled
me here with a
two-inch cable.
I'm taking you
out of this side
show ... You're
coming with me
as my wife ... in
the eyes of God,
and man, and the
United States
Passport Bureau."

—Robert Taylor
as Bill

LADY OF THE TROPICS
HEDY LAMARR
AND
ROBERT TAYLOR
1939

No man could ever find a cure for the lure of Tondelayo!

(ABOVE)
WHITE CARGO
HEDY LAMARR
AND
WALTER PIDGEON
1942

(LEFT)
WHITE CARGO
HEDY LAMARR
AND
RICHARD CARLSON
1942

(they kiss)

MARAMA:

I worry about everything when you're away. About the wind.
About the waves. Sometimes I worry that fish eat you up.

TERANGI:

Me? You worry about me? Why, I'm the best sailor
in the whole world!

MARAMA:

I know.

TERANGI:

I'm the best swimmer, too.

MARAMA:

I know.

TERANGI:

And tonight when we come out of the church, oh Marama,
I'm the best husband in the whole world.

MARAMA:

I know. I know.

TERANGI:

Shut up. You don't know anything yet!

THE HURRICANE
DOROTHY LAMOUR AND JON HALL
1937

TERRY:

Please open the door. Please.

EDIE:

I want you to stay away from me!

(he breaks through the door)

TERRY:

I know what you want me to do, but I ain't going to do it, so forget about it!

EDIE:

I don't want you to do anything! You let your conscience tell you what to do.

TERRY:

Shut up about that conscience! That's all I've been hearing!

EDIE:

I never mentioned the word before. You just stay away from me!

TERRY:

Edie, I—Edie, you love me.

EDIE:

I didn't say I didn't love you. I said stay away from me.

TERRY:

I want you to say it to me.

EDIE:

Stay away from me.

(they kiss)

ON THE WATERFRONT
MARLON BRANDO AND EVA MARIE SAINT
1954

SOME OF THE ACTRESSES GABLE KISSED DURING HIS CAREER:

MARY ASTOR

CARROLL BAKER

CONSTANCE BENNETT

CLAUDETTE COLBERT

JOAN CRAWFORD

MARION DAVIES

DORIS DAY

YVONNE DE CARLO

MADGE EVANS

GRETA GARBO

AVA GARDNER

GREER GARSON

JEAN HARLOW

HELEN HAYES

SUSAN HAYWARD

GRACE KELLY

DEBORAH KERR

HEDY LAMARR

VIVIEN LEIGH

CAROLE LOMBARD

BLACKIE

*You know, Mary, I want to get a kick out of things I can see,
like lights in the harbor, or a good fight, or a woman worth looking at.
Did you ever taste the fog in your mouth like it was salt? Or take hold of
someone and feel your blood rushing up like a river? What more does a
man need, or a woman either? You know I never tried to kid you,
Mary. You take me as I am or you don't take me. Tim doesn't try to change
you because he knows he can't. And you can't either. Nothing can.
Do you know what I've been waiting for? I've been waiting to hear you
say that I'm all right with you the way I am.
Maybe you're ready to say it now. Are you?*

MARY
I don't know.

BLACKIE
Well, it's about time.

(they kiss)

SAN FRANCISCO
CLARK GABLE AND JEANETTE MACDONALD
1936

DENNIS
Come here.

VANTINE
Why, Mr. Carson!

DENNIS
Come here, you lug.

VANTINE
Well, it's about time!

*(He pulls her onto his lap.
They kiss.)*

VANTINE
Welcome home, senator.

(they kiss)

(they kiss)

BARBARA
We shouldn't have done that.

DENNIS
We did.

(they kiss. She breaks away.)

MICHAEL
Why, hello.

SALLY
Hello.

(they kiss)

SALLY
You know, I've known people I've liked and some I've disliked. I've hated a few and thought I loved a couple, but I've never known anyone I could trust up to now.

RED DUST
CLARK GABLE AND JEAN HARLOW
1932

RED DUST
MARY ASTOR AND CLARK GABLE
1932

LOVE ON THE RUN
JOAN CRAWFORD AND CLARK GABLE
1936

CANDY
Have you any idea what a gal like you can do to a gent like me?

ELIZABETH
I'd like to know. Tell me.

CANDY
Well, I've seen women I'd look at quicker but never one I'd look at longer.

ELIZABETH
Well, that's a good start. Go on.

CANDY
I could put you in my vest pocket and lose you in the small change. And me—now I've always gone for women with something to 'em. The kind that could stand up and slug it out with me toe to toe. You slug me just by looking at me.

HONKY TONK
CLARK GABLE AND LANA TURNER
1941

"Grief ain't
what I came
after. You got
class, kid. Or
is it because I
haven't seen
any women
lately."

CLARK GABLE
STRANGE CARGO
1940

ACE
How much do you love me?

JAN
*How much? Let me see how much. Well, it's about
ten feet high and about seven feet wide.*

ACE
Never mind that.

JAN
Oh, I can't measure it now. It's a storm at sea.

(they kiss)

ACE
You do love me, don't you?

JAN
It's madness, nothing else.

A FREE SOUL
NORMA SHEARER AND CLARK GABLE
1931

MIKE: Tracy.

TRACY: What do you want?

MIKE: You're wonderful.

TRACY: Ha ha ha ha ha ha ha ha ha.

MIKE: There's a magnificence in you, Tracy... a magnificence that comes out of your eyes and your voice and the way that you stand there and the way you walk. You're lit from within, Tracy. You've got fires banked down in you. Hearth fires and holocausts.

TRACY: I don't seem to you made of bronze?

MIKE: No, you're made out of flesh and blood. That's the blank unholy surprise of it. Oh, you're the golden girl, Tracy. Full of life and warmth and delight... Oh, what goes on? You've got tears in your eyes.

TRACY: Shut up. Shut up. Oh, Mike, keep talking, keep talking. Talk, will you?
(they kiss)

TRACY: Golly...
(they kiss)

TRACY: Golly molly. Mr. Conner. Mr. Conner.

MIKE: Tracy. Tracy. Let me tell you something, Tracy.

TRACY: No, don't. All of a sudden I've got the shakes.

MIKE: It can't be anything like love, can it?

TRACY: No, no. It mustn't be. It can't.

MIKE: Would it be inconvenient?

TRACY: Terribly. Anyway, I know it isn't. Oh, Mike, we're out of our minds...

MIKE: And right into our hearts... Tracy, you're tremendous.

TRACY: That's funny, because I feel very small. Put me in your pocket, Mike.

THE PHILADELPHIA STORY
KATHARINE HEPBURN AND JAMES STEWART
1940

COUNT:

Stay a moment. When the door closes upon you, I shall doubt that
all this really happened. You're here beside me. If I bend my head, I
can feel your cheek against my lips and I can
hear your voice saying incredible things.
Have you ever thought that people to whom miracles happen
must be a little dazed. The blind man to whom
sight is suddenly given must be startled by the strange new world.
So it is with me. I came here hoping to catch a glimpse of you at court.
You might have flung me a word, gracious and
indifferent as you passed. Instead . . .

(they kiss; a bell starts to ring)

MARIE:

Listen. The village is waking.

COUNT:

I must let you go. Goodbye.

MARIE:

Good night. Or, if you wish, good morning. I shall never say
goodbye.

(they kiss)

MARIE ANTOINETTE
TYRONE POWER AND NORMA SHEARER
1938

CHAPTER THREE

COMMITMENT

You must remember this:

A kiss is still a kiss; a sigh is just a sigh.

The fundamental things apply

As time goes by.

And when two lovers woo, they still say, "I love you."

On that you can rely;

No matter what the future brings,

As time goes by.

(LEFT)
DAVID COPPERFIELD
MAUREEN O'SULLIVAN AND FRANK LAWTON
1934

(ABOVE)
CASABLANCA
INGRID BERGMAN AND HUMPHREY BOGART
1942

This song of
the Man and his Wife
is of no place
and every place;
you might hear it anywhere
at any time.
Wherever the sun rises and sets
in the City's turmoil
or under the open sky on the farm
life is much the same;
sometimes bitter,
sometimes sweet.

—DIALOGUE CARD

SUNRISE
JANET GAYNOR AND GEORGE O'BRIEN
1927

JIM: Melisande!

MELISANDE: Jimmee!

(they kiss)

THE BIG PARADE
RENEE ADOREE AND JOHN GILBERT
1925

MR. DARCY:

I can struggle against you no longer.

ELIZABETH:

Mr. Darcy!

MR. DARCY:

*I've reminded myself again and again that I have obligations to family and position . . .
obligations I was born to. Nothing that I tell myself matters. I love you. I love you.*
(he kisses her hand)

ELIZABETH:

Do you know what you're saying?

MR. DARCY:

Yes, my darling. I'm asking you to marry me.

ELIZABETH:

*Do you expect me to thank you for this extraordinary offer of marriage? Am I supposed to feel flattered
that you have so overcome your aversion to my family that you are ready to marry into it?*

TIME HAS PASSED

ELIZABETH:

Oh, Mr. Darcy. When I think of how I've misjudged you, the horrible things I said . . . I'm so ashamed.

MR. DARCY:

*Oh, no. It is I who should be ashamed . . . of my arrogance, of my stupid pride, of it all—except one thing.
One thing. I'm not ashamed of having loved you . . . Elizabeth, dare I ask you again?*
(she smiles and nods)

MR. DARCY:

Elizabeth, dear beautiful Lizzy . . .
(they kiss)

PRIDE AND PREJUDICE
GREER GARSON AND LAURENCE OLIVIER
1940

TRACY: Dexter, are you sure?

DEXTER: Not in the least, but I'll risk it. Will you?

TRACY: You bet. You didn't do it just to soften the blow?

DEXTER: No, Tracy.

TRACY: Nor to save my face?

DEXTER: Oh, it's a nice little face.

TRACY: Never in my life have I been so full of love before.

THE PHILADELPHIA STORY
CARY GRANT AND KATHARINE HEPBURN
1940

SAM:
Something I've got to get off my chest.

TESS:
I'm too heavy?

SAM:
I love you.

TESS:
Me, too.

SAM:
Positive.

TESS:
That's nice. Even when I'm sober?

SAM:
Even when you're brilliant.

(they kiss)

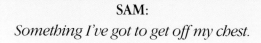

WOMAN OF THE YEAR
KATHARINE HEPBURN AND SPENCER TRACY
1942

You better be nice to me, or I'll take my trailer and go home.

Like me. No good without you.

Well, I'll tell you a secret.
Your trailer is no good
without my car to haul it.

THE LONG
LONG TRAILER
DESI ARNAZ
AND
LUCILLE BALL
1954

It's very clear,

Our love is here to stay.

Not for a year,

But ever and a day.

The radio and the telephone

And the movies that we know

May just be passing fancies,

And in time may go.

But oh, my dear,

Our love is here to stay;

Together we're going a long, long way.

In time the Rockies may crumble,

Gibralter may tumble,

They're only made of clay,

But our love is here to stay.

AN AMERICAN IN PARIS
LESLIE CARON AND GENE KELLY
1951

GEORGE: What is it that you want, Mary? What do you want? You want the moon? I'll throw a lasso around it and pull it down. Hey, that's a pretty good idea! I'll give you the moon, Mary. **MARY:** I'll take it...then what?

GEORGE: Well, then you  could swallow it, and it'd all dissolve, see? And the moonbeams'd come out of your hair—am I talking too much? **GUY ON A BALCONY:** Yes! Why don't you kiss her instead of talking her to death? **GEORGE:** How's that? **GUY:** Why don't you kiss her instead of talking her to death! **GEORGE:** You want me to kiss her, huh? **GUY:** Oh! Youth is wasted on the wrong people! **GEORGE:** Hey, hey mister! Come back out here! I'll show you a kiss that'll put hair back on your head!

IT'S A WONDERFUL LIFE
DONNA REED AND JAMES STEWART
1946

While I give to you
and you give to me
True love, true love.
So, on and on it will
always be
True love, true love.
For you and I have
a guardian
angel on high
With nothing to do
But to give to you
and to give to me
Love forever true.

NICK: Mommy, let's sit down.

NORA: Sit down? What for?

NICK: Just to get a little rest after
our quiet weekend
in the country.
(they kiss)

ANOTHER THIN MAN
MYRNA LOY AND WILLIAM POWELL
1939

CHAPTER FOUR

FOREVER

NORMAN:

Hello, there.

ETHEL:

Hi.

NORMAN:

Wanna dance or do you just want to suck face?

(LEFT)
MODERN TIMES
CHARLES CHAPLIN AND PAULETTE GODDARD
1936

(ABOVE)
ON GOLDEN POND
HENRY FONDA AND KATHARINE HEPBURN
1981

COPYRIGHTS AND CREDITS

In cases where excerpts from the screenplay of a film appear in the text, the screenwriters have been credited in addition to any novel, play, etc. from which the screenplay has been adapted. All copyright notices are for the films unless otherwise noted.

THE BRIBE *Ava Gardner and Robert Taylor 1949*

18–19: LOVE FINDS ANDY HARDY

ANDY HARDY MEETS A DEBUTANTE

GIRL CRAZY

Screenplay by Fred Finklehoffe. Based on the play by Guy Bolton and Jack McGowan.

20–21: BABES ON BROADWAY

Screenplay by Fred Finklehoffe and Elaine Ryan.

22–23: ZIEGFELD GIRL

LITTLE NELLIE KELLY

Screenplay by Jack McGowan. Based on the play by George M. Cohan.

24–25: CABIN IN THE SKY

Honey In The Honeycomb lyrics by John LaTouche

26–27: THE DIVORCEE

Screenplay by Zelda Sears, Nick Grinde, and John Meehan. Based on the novel *Ex-Wife* by Ursula Parrott.

28–29: RANDOM HARVEST

Screenplay by Claudine West, George Froeschel, and Arthur Wimperis. Based on the novel by James Hilton.

30–31: TARZAN AND HIS MATE

Screenplay by James Kevin McGuiness. Adaptation by Howard Emmett Rogers and Leon Gordon.

TARZAN ESCAPES

32–35: ROMEO AND JULIET

Screenplay by Talbot Jennings. Based on the play by William Shakespeare.

BEN HUR *Carmel Myers and Ramon Novarro 1925*

INDEX

JEZEBEL *Bette Davis and Henry Fonda 1938*

AS YOU DESIRE ME *Greta Garbo and Erich von Stroheim 1932*

✦ CRYSTAL ✦

...Oh, if this could just go on forever.

✦ RAYMOND ✦

Well, all good things must come to an end.

You know that.

✦ CRYSTAL ✦

Is that original?

✦ RAYMOND ✦

No, but it's true, unfortunately.

AS YOU DESIRE ME *Greta Garbo and Erich von Stroheim 1932*

♦ CRYSTAL ♦
…Oh, if this could just go on forever.

♦ RAYMOND ♦
Well, all good things must come to an end.

You know that.

♦ CRYSTAL ♦
Is that original?

♦ RAYMOND ♦
No, but it's true, unfortunately.

(ABOVE AND PAGE 1)
PERSONAL PROPERTY
JEAN HARLOW
AND
ROBERT TAYLOR
1937